WAX

Poems of Identity and Impermanence

CISSY STAG

Dedication

To Iris, who flickers but never fades.
To Daisy, who loves in permanence.
To Mara, who carries history like armor.
To Ivy, who runs fast and burns bright.
To Luna, who follows the glow, even in the dark.
To Blue, who dances where the world is quiet.

And to Cissy, who is all of them,
melting, shifting, becoming,
but this time, staying.

And of course, to my favorite people.
You know who you are.

Introduction

Hi. I'm Cissy. I began writing *Wax* when my sense of self felt like something molten, constantly shifting, never quite solid. My second psychotic episode happened on the anniversary of my first, as if to remind me how fragile identity can be. Psychosis strips you bare, reshapes you in ways you never expected. It is both destruction and reinvention, a fire you survive but never walk away from unchanged.

Wax: Poems of Identity & Impermanence is about that fire. It's about how life, through trauma, love, loss, melts away the parts of us that once felt permanent. It's about transformation, about what remains after the burn.

For a long time, I thought impermanence was all there was. That nothing could last. That love, identity, and stability would always slip through my fingers. But as I wrote, I realized something: wax doesn't just melt; it sets again. Fire doesn't just destroy; it clears space for something new.

This book is not just about loss. It is about choosing what stays.

I hope these poems help you find your own shape in the fire.

Table of Contents

Wax

How do you think we'll be remembered?
Will the town raise statues in our honor?

No?

What about Madame Tussaud?
Will her ghost recreate our figures for all to admire?

Here stands Cissy Stag.
5'5".
Taller in heels... and bad at math...

Will she capture the look in my eyes?
If so, which one?

Sadness?
Anger?
Fear?

What about the glimmer in my eyes?
You know the one.

On nights when my pupils grow large,
And the stars shine much brighter...

What about my irises?
Will they be rich like amber or just... brown?

Part of Your World

Sometimes...
I feel like you're a figment of my imagination.
I can see it.
Us.
Together.

Holding hands in a field of irises after a controlled burn.
They are beautiful.

I reach out and clasp your hand...
And there are like...
A LOT of fingers...
You should probably see a doctor about that...

I laugh it off,
And I accept it as my reality.

I'm sorry, ya know?
For making you my muse.
Someone to use.
I did it because you are beautiful...
And you saw something in me that I didn't see myself...

But truly... it brings me blues...
On nights like these.
When I feel a little bit like a normal girl...
And all I want is to tell my secrets...

That Old Adage

They say that love is blind.
I cannot say that I agree:
Love sees what it wants to see.

Offering

I love you.
You know that, right?

They say that love is subjective,
And I think that's what makes loving you so rewarding.

I love learning about you...
What triggers you.
What makes you smile.
What makes you cry...
Happy tears.

I love you for your brain.
I love you for your playfulness.
I love you because you hold space for people like you...
And people unlike you.

I love you because you love the simple things:
Animals. Tea. Tarot. Plants. Dance. Movies. TV.

I love seeing you succeed.
I love being proud of you.
I love it when you are proud of yourself.
And proud of your people.

I love my weird little life,
And the weird little stories that I have...
All because I met you.

She was the death of my marriage
And the rebirth of my life...
With just a simple offering:
A snakeskin.

I love the life born of my biography,
Born of bloodshed.
Because it's a life where I learned to love deeply,
Compassionately.
And hold space for people to just be...
People.

If I could go back, and unmeet her... would I?
No.

Because my life is rich with love,
And I wouldn't be me now if I hadn't met her then.

Thank you for trusting me.
I love to see you burn bright.
And Blue.

Unrequited

I could be the love of your life if you let me.
But you don't.

I love you unconditionally.
There.
I said it.

My love for you knows no boundaries,
Except for the boundaries that you set,
So, I respect them.

The thing about my love
Is that I am okay with it being unrequited.
You do not have to love me
For me to love you.
I just do.

Because love is subjective,
And you are objectively lovable.

You're a player,
And so am I.
I am the best player in the game.
Because I am playful...
And when it comes down to it...
I don't care which role you play in my life.

Your presence is enough for me.
Always has been.
Always will be.

The Study

Where do you think we'll be when they come for us?
No.
Not those clowns.
Or the feds.
We're too hot and funny for that.
Besides, they have charismatic cult leaders to catch.

So, you think that we'll rule the world?
Or will we give up on it?
Phone our people.
Take us home.

Home that lies between the constellations...
The big burning balls of fire in the sky...

Think that we'll remember their language when they arrive?
Or will we shut our mouths and dance...?
Like good dancers do.

Will we see The Great Pyramids from space?
Will they show us Aurora Borealis on our way out?
Do you think we'll be fine without oxygen after screaming
our lungs out?
Surely, we have grown gills by now...
Or better...
Cloacas.

When we leave this place,
Will we leave this timeline?

Inhale.
Exhale.
I guess we'll find out.

Could be tomorrow.
But probably not.

After all, I promised to live a long life...
Because that's what I want.

Sometimes... old wounds still ache.
That's all.
In time, the inflammation will die down...
And it will just be... easy.
Almost... as if it never happened.

James Marie

Revelations spoke of The Anti-Christ...
I never thought that I'd be The One.

Red hair.
Brown eyes.
Freckles.
Always a swimmer.
Never a runner...
Until my blood and body spilled over dinner.

The Prophecy spoke of the coming of Christ...
I bet they weren't counting on it to be her...
5'7"... 6'3" in heels.

And me...?
Well... let's just say
I know her name isn't James Marie...

Ice of Providence

What would it take to buy your silence?
Two thousand bitcoin?
A threat made against you and your loved ones...?

Would you stay silent,
Hoping to keep them safe?
Or would you scream
Until you no longer could?

His irises matched ice,
And I knew...
He wasn't what he showed the world.
Not a family man...
A monster,
Unwilling to break a cycle of abuse.

I fought for my life last December.
Believed everything to be delusions...
And wished to remember no longer.

Ice...
That's what fills my lungs
With blind eyes and deformed hands
As I choke on the silence
Of a life-or-death situation.

One...
Two...

Michael Birch

I love you.
There.
I said it.

I never thought you to be real...
Only a hallucination.
Faux.
An illusion.

I loved you before I knew your identity...
And now...
I know.
And I don't know what to do with it.

I loved your wife the most.
FOREVER.

So...
What do I make of this?
An unlikely confession
That I shared with her,
Under the assumption that she knew.

But she didn't.
She retreated to the girls
Who continue to abuse me.

So, what do I do?
Is it wrong that I fell in love then?
Is it wrong that I forgive him now
For indiscretions worse than anyone else's...
Just because he was honest?

Mead

Last night,
I let go.

Professed my love in privacy
Over a soft pretzel and too much mead.

In the moment,
I was surrounded by real people.
As my blood tainted,
My mind retreated into itself...
And I let it.

And then I sent one last text.
A test.
To confirm with his silence
That a crush is just a crush.

And I sent another...
To the man I met online...
To give it another shot.

Their irises flickered
To the sound of my heartbeat,
But it wasn't enough.

Last night,
I let go of my favorite people...
Because I am done with casual cruelty.

Choose love.
I did.

I'm running headfirst into this new life...
One where I am accepted for my darkness,

My light,
And everything in between.

Far from the grounds of The Haunted House.
My world is not black and white.
I see all the colors now.

At the Museum...

Am I a visitor?
...or am I on display?

Do you see me in wax?
Frozen in time,
A figure to admire,
Or simply to pass by?

Stained

What's that on my shirt?

Blood?
Wine?
Lipstick?
Wax?

Taste it...
Tell me...

Does it linger?
Sweet, bitter, metallic?
Does it burn,
Or does it fade?

Thanksgiving

Where were you when the Anti-Christ arrived?
Were you driving?
Were you gathered around the table,
Stuffing yourself with meats and fats,
Drinking yourself blind?

Did you even notice the coming of Christ?
Did you see the lights?
Or did you brush it off as a hallucination?

They say that only men become prophets...
But perhaps women are the deities
The prophets foretold.

Born of bloodshed.
One rib.
A taste for knowledge.
And a serpent.

When fire rains, we will not be absent.
We'll be there.
And this time...
It will be a controlled burn.

The Magic

"...the magic just... isn't there..."
That's what he said when I asked him if he loved her.

I've been fixated for a while now...
On his eyes.
His smile.
His body language.

The way he grows cold, like stone...
And then gives me that look...
You know the one.

Until I sense his heat,
Warm enough to approach.

Six months...
That's how long it's been
Since I first laid eyes on him.

Is it wrong of me to still be holding out hope?
Six months.
Four fallouts.
Countless misunderstandings.

But then there's that feeling...
You know the one.

Sometimes, the magic just... isn't there.
But I've never felt that way in his presence.

The magic has always been there.
I just fear the magic is... unrequited.

The Woods

My mind wanders between dreams...
Hopes.
Fears.
Delusions.
Fantasies.

And the reality
That is pieced together with a bit of each.

I ponder the idea of soulmates...
Invisible strings.
Magic.
Things that are meant to be...
And things that are not...

Do you feel real after all of this?
Or do you feel like me?
Sketched.
A figment of someone's imagination...

Gentle Pressures

Last night,
I dreamed that you responded...
You texted me back...

Isn't the human psyche strange?
Of all the desires to be explored...

Breathing on my neck...
Nuzzling my ear...
Cradling my skull in your hands...
Wiping sweat from my brow...

Burying your head in my chest,
And sneaking a bite so that I shriek with joy...
Allowing your body to lie on mine...
Dominating me through gentle pressures.
Skin to skin.
Drawing your fingertips down my core and past my navel
ring...

Grabbing my hips as if letting them go
Would result in your descent to the underworld.
Pulling me closer...
And closer...

Until one of us screams with relief,
And then the other does, too.

Isn't it stranger
How the mind can acknowledge all these desires,
And still boost a simple response to the forefront?

Beyond the gentle pressures
And not so gentle ones,
My deepest desire is acknowledgment.

Stillness

The lake is a dark mirror,
Cradled in navy skies.
Stars whisper their truths,
Scattering light across still waters.

Ducks murmur softly,
Their voices fading
Into the night's embrace.

I stand on wooden lattice,
A shadow swaying gently,
Breathing in the quiet.

Reflected peace glimmers...
A fleeting truth,
Before dawn stretches,
Spilling light across the lake.

In this stillness,
I wait.

Intimate Photos

My intuition told me to do it.
Bare my heart.
My soul.
My body...

The fruits of my labor.
My secrets.
In a private gallery.

I don't know what happened last year...
But I cannot help but think
That my privacy was violated in ways unspeakable.

So, the unspeakables have been recorded.
Documented.
Stored with everything else.

And if they remain private,
That's swell.
It's how it should be.

But if they don't...

My cup will overflow with secrets,
Leaking all over the screens,
The hearts,
The souls,
The eyes
Of everyone who doubted me
When I said it happened to me.

Is my heart tainted?
Or has it merely departed?

Miscommunications

I never meant to break your heart.
I hope you know that.

I saw the glimmer in your eye fade...
And like an apparition, you were gone.

How many times can one heart fracture
Over missed opportunities and miscommunications?
How many times can you grow angry at an ex-lover
For ignoring your cries when all you wanted was them?
In any role in your life.

It didn't bring me joy to deliver the news.
It broke me.

Because I picked you
Over, and over, and over again...
And it still wasn't enough.

It's no secret.
I'm still fixated.
And he picked me anyway.

Crazy...
Everybody seems to agree that I am.
But he says I don't seem that crazy...
All things considered.

Tattoos

People often ask when I'll move on...
I don't know.
How long would it take you to move on?

From trauma and connections
That feel written in the stars?
From moments so grand,
You tattoo them onto your body
Just to stay tethered to this world?

Is it really that simple?
A miscommunication lacking nuance?
Or does it run deeper than that...?

Through the darkness...
The skies...
The moon...
And the stars that align.

Do you not believe in magic?

And let's say the magic isn't there...
Let's say the divine signs
Are nothing more than coincidences.

Does that make you feel better?
Happier?
Healthier?
Saner?

Or does it just... disappoint you?

Lighthouse

His irises matched my headboard,
And that was enough.

Enough for me to idealize him despite his flaws,
And allow every lover after him to simply... fade away.

His irises matched my headboard,
And I always saw him as a beacon of hope.
A lighthouse.
Despite the midnight skies and tumultuous waves of his
darkness.

His irises matched my headboard,
And I never once regretted my fixation on him.
His body.
His mind.
His soul.
His heart.

And all the things that make him eccentric...
Like me.

Have you been to the bottom of the sea?
Just to float back up,
But never know how to break the surface tension?
I have.

His irises matched my headboard,
And that was enough.

Enough for me to drown out the whispers of admiration
From anyone who wasn't him.

Between Breaths

Beyond the fracture lines of sanity's mask,
We spin through shattered spheres,
Our silhouettes bound by threads of light.
An infinite dance across fragile glass,
Mapping stars in the fractures of time.

In the quiet of this cosmos,
I sense your name,
Entwined with Blue's,
A resonance that hums through dissociation,
Dark and glittering,
Unfolding in the spaces between.

Beneath the weight of cosmic silence,
We carry the memory of what it means
To stand amidst the irises,
Their petals like whispers of forgotten skies.

Do we break the glass, or let it hold us?
Do we walk through the field,
Or let the horizon swallow us whole?

Perhaps the answer lies not in movement,
But in the stillness between breaths...
In the glow of the shards,
The hum of flowers,
The way the universe bends to listen
When we call it home.

Wide Enough for Galaxies

"What does magic feel like?"
I wanted to ask,
but his face was already tilted upward,
searching the sky for something
he couldn't name.

The night pressed close,
its silence loud enough
to hold the words
we were too afraid to speak.

I didn't know if I was jealous of her
or of his distance...
the way he drifted just beyond my reach,
an orbit I couldn't escape.

The tailgate groaned under our weight,
but the stars held theirs without question.
We sat in their glow,
small and infinite at once,
wrapped in a fragile thread of unspoken truths.

The space between us
was wide enough for galaxies
and still too narrow to hide
how much I wanted
to pull him closer.

Type O

At the theater,
I see him.

The immortal beast who feasts on blood,
Aches for her heart.
And in that moment,
I grew... bored.

His eternal longing echoed.
A shadow of feelings I once knew.
The one with visions and nightmares,
Confusing love for the demon who hunts.

In time, obsession has faded.
Where deep lacerations of hypervigilance once cut,
Now mere scars remain...
Noticeable, yet
Easy to cover with a tattoo.

Beyond Her

Don't bother washing your sheets.
I have a better idea.
Wrap me in the scent of your other lovers.

Sink your teeth into my neck.
Inhale her memory
From the pillow beneath my hips.

Strip me bare.
Apply gentle pressure
On my wounded dignity.

Bury yourself in me.
Deep enough to fear
Hitting Earth's core.

Bite my top lip
As you grow tense,
Breathe in deeply...
Every moment you lived... behind her.

Look me in my eyes.
Wipe my brow.
Think of every time you consumed her...
How you missed me most,
Then release.

Iris

If we're being honest with each other...
Lover to lover.
Favorite person to favorite person.

I think my love for you is not unrequited.
I think you're just afraid...
Not of me, but of everyone I roared at in my defense
As they picked apart my trauma,
Violated my boundaries,
And blamed me for their decisions...
Including contacting her.

I defend you in your absence because I love you,
But I love me more.

And as I witness your continued support for those
Who preferred to keep me isolated,
As I barely clung to life...

It becomes clear to me
That you will continue to choose them over me...
Always desire me, but never fully claim me.

Because if you did,
You would need to defend me in my absence.
And I'm not sure you love yourself enough to do that.

The smallest thing once held power.
His irises matched my headboard,
And that was enough for me.

Enough to love him still,
In hopes he'd finally see my value
And claim me... fiercely, unapologetically...

Iris Again

I made myself go back to sleep to deal with my anger
And woke to his year in review.

There was a time in my life
When I believed torturing him was justified.
Not because I hated him,
But because I was afraid of losing him.

Not a relationship or a friendship.
Him. His life.

So, I tortured him.
Manipulated him.
Made him angry.

Because I remembered what it felt like
To be at the bottom of The Well,
Wanting to surrender my life entirely.

And how I only started climbing
When I became angry enough to choose myself.

Residual anger towards him still haunts my soul
As I learn to manage my triggers
From the pain caused by those around him.

His irises matched my headboard,
And that was enough.

Enough for me to show him
The worst parts of myself...
Hoping he'd learn to love himself enough to stay.

NYE

Sometimes, I forget that we're not together.
I certainly forgot last night.

While scratching your back
Like a stylus reading a record,
Using your rhythm
Like my personal drum set.

Toying with your movement
As if you were my puppet.
Dancing with you.

And in a moment of euphoria,
Resting my chin on your shoulder
As if you were mine.

Sometimes, I forget...
Because the moments feel natural.

The pendant around my neck
Is no longer the little T-rex.
It's a crescent moon with a rabbit.

I showed it to you,
And you said, "I love it."
And in that moment,
I forgot that we're not together.

Through the Arc to Midnight

There's a pattern to our unraveling...
A rhythm traced not on skin,
But through fabric and proximity.
A dance of almosts,
Charged with an emotional undercurrent
That lingers in the space between breaths.

I drew maps on you,
Pressing meaning into the threads of your button-up shirt,
My hands speaking truths my mouth couldn't.
You leaned closer,
Words grazing my ear...
A soft collision of sound and intent,
The weight of your voice pulling me in.

This wasn't touch as they know it,
But the kind that lives in the pause,
In the tilt of a head,
The brush of breath against hair...
A silent language only we understood.

And yet, even in that moment,
The air carried the weight of goodbye.
A reminder that this closeness
Was destined to fade.

Midnight came,
And you had already slipped away,
Your absence sharper than any distance.

Still, I stayed.
Replaying the rhythm of our nearness,
The heat of words left unspoken,
The maps I traced on your presence,

Knowing the night itself was foreplay
For the longing to follow.

Worthy Enough

I have carried myself
Through the weight of silence,
Pushing against the walls
Of unspoken inequities.

For more than a year,
I've stood alone.
In the stillness of my own care,
Where no hands reached to hold,
And no voice spoke softly
Of sanctuary.

But now,
There is a fire beneath my ribs,
A quiet rebellion in my chest...
A demand for something greater.
Not a shelter forged by others' hands,
But a kingdom I can call my own.

I will not return to the echoes
Of dependency,
Nor surrender to the shame
That whispers I should wait...
To be chosen,
To be saved.

This is my voice,
Raw as an open wound,
Declaring:
I am more than enough.

Not as a wife,
Or a lover,
But as myself.

And though the world
May not see my worth,
I will keep shouting into the void,
Carving my place
From the hollows of doubt.

One day,
The silence will break,
And it will not be their applause
I hear,
But my own song,
Rising.

Most of All

I love you.
You must know that by now.

Despite the ways
I become eccentric when I am angry,
I want you to know how much I care.

About you.
Your boundaries.
Your comfort.
Your happiness.

And yes,
I hope my hopes for you are self-serving...
That you will reciprocate.
Hold me.
Love me.
Fuck me.
Stay with me.
Understand me.

But most of all,
When I love,
I REALLY love.

You.
Most of all.

Not for Him

I washed his scent from my sheets one last time,
Just like I did before.
But this time,
I meant it.

"He doesn't want to spend time with you like I do."
His words nearly burned me alive,
Spoken an hour after I last saw my muse.

Ignorance.
A knife to the heart,
Though he didn't know
He was holding a prop as he took aim.

She Sent Me Flowers Today

She sent me flowers today:
Roses wrapped in ivy,
Hydrangeas heavy with the scent
Of something sweeter,
Something stolen.

The ivy crept first,
Twisting around my doorframe,
Its tendrils whispering secrets
I didn't ask to hear.
It pulled at the cracks in my walls,
Testing their strength,
Prying them open
To let Mara in.

Mara arrived like a shadow...
A quiet storm of bitterness and need,
Her voice soft as petals
But sharp as thorns.
She claimed the garden was hers,
And the ivy seemed to agree.

But still, the roses bloomed,
Their crimson heads lifted
Like tiny suns defying the dark.
And the hydrangeas...
Oh, the hydrangeas!
They spilled across the soil,
A cascade of lavender laughter,
Unafraid of Mara's shadow.

She sent me flowers today,
But I chose to keep the ones
That danced in the light.

Roses for their unyielding fire,
Hydrangeas for their quiet joy.

And though the ivy clings still,
Its roots searching for purchase,
It cannot choke what grows freely...
What grows for me.

She sent me flowers today,
And I learned to tend my own garden.

Petals in the Snow

Everyone gets their karma,
And sometimes,
Their karma is seeing me happy...
Like a rose in the snow,
Bright and warm
In a sea of cold souls.

I saw flowers today
On the streets of Atlanta,
Coated in ice but still vibrant.
Pink, yellow, blue.

While the snow turned to gray slurry,
And the streets forgot their wonder,
The petals remained through the flurry.

DeKalb County

We'd have packed our lives into boxes of dreams,
Left behind the gulf and its restless extremes.
Decatur's heat would still hum through the air,
A blue house standing, steady and spare.

Insurance calls would fill the days,
The kind of grind that keeps fears at bay.
No watchers lurking, no cracks in the glass,
No tethered past pulling shadows to pass.

Echeveria would still claim her throne,
Her tiny hops through a yard we'd own.
The stage would have whispered, a casual affair,
No trauma laced in the laughter there.

Yet even then, in that life of ease,
Would the quiet have truly pleased?
Would the calm, so sure, the nights so plain,
Have quenched your thirst... or left you drained?

For here in the chaos, the scars took root,
Blooming as books, as art, as truth.
The dark carved you, the pain refined,
A richer hue in the threads that bind.

Would you trade the fire for safer ground,
For a love unchallenged, neatly wound?
For a quiet life of unbroken rest,
Would you have denied yourself the test?

DeKalb County hums of might-have-beens,
Of lives unwritten, uncarved within.
But this life, this chaos, with its jagged hue,
Was made for a soul as fierce as you.

I Left Her Books Today

I left her books today:
a box folded loosely,
its edges pressed together
just enough to hold
what was already spilling over.

The spines lay uneven,
their corners worn thin,
their ink a whisper
of truths buried within.

I left them at the garden gate,
for the watcher who grew...
who will push it open,
scatter the words like seeds,
and tend them in soil
where her roots can deepen,
and blooms might rise
from ash and stone.

And for the other...
the one who circles and prods,
her hands brushing the edges
of what she denies...
the books will sit in shadow,
their weight ignored,
but their roots pressing deeper,
beyond her reach.

I left her books today,
not folded neatly,
because life never is,
and the words had already been planted
where her child still lives.

For the watcher who grew,
they are a garden of play,
each bloom a reminder
that growth lights the way.
For the watcher who refused,
they are shadows untold,
truths left unopened,
her garden grown cold.

And when I rest,
when the soil holds my frame,
the child I once was
will return to the same.
The garden will bloom
where innocence stands,
its roots holding steady
in small, eager hands.

The words will remain,
in their soil they'll stay,
preserving the lessons
that taught us to play.

Enough

The city was always magic,
long before his irises caught my attention.
His irises matched my headboard, and that was enough.
Enough for me to want to get better.

In seven days, new love had come and gone.
And then it returned.
Again.
And again.
And again.

Each time, it looked a little different.
Sometimes sadder.
Sometimes angrier.
And then one day, it returned like a slow bloom,
deeply cared for...
the petals of new trust unfolding in quiet reverence.

His irises matched my headboard, and that was enough.
Enough for me to commit to his peace,
to my peace.

Because even in the darkest moments,
when the city's magic seemed to fade,
his presence was always enough
to keep the magic alive.

I Save Her Pictures in My Phone

I save her pictures in my phone:
Tangible evidence of growth,
Prosperity,
Freedom.
A complete 180 from the way I found her,
Months after the split.

Sometimes, I get jealous,
Because my growth hasn't brought me
The success that's found her.
But I love to see it anyway.

I save her pictures in my phone
To remind myself:
I invested my energy wisely.
No drop in a puddle,
But a wave in the ocean...
Flowing freely,
Bright,
And Blue.

Unattainable

Am I the bad girl of your dreams,
or the good girl haunting your nightmares?
Let's keep this secret.
I know you like it that way.
Quiet.
Subtle.
Your vitriol tied in little details,
each word a thread
leading straight to my bed.

Tell me,
how badly do you ache for me?
Is it enough to unravel the truth:
that I'm untouched,
but never out of reach for you?

His Irises Matched My Headboard

I wrote of him to make her jealous.
And it worked.

Her role as my muse slowly faded;
she became ready... willing... to intervene
when it didn't work out with him and me.
She'd find me heartbroken,
and build me back up,
roast by roast:
of me, of her, of everyone else.
And I adore her for that.

It's hard, you know?
To have the capacity to love
and to be queer,
but never really know what that means for you.

His irises matched my headboard,
and that was enough...
enough for me to tell my girlfriend it was over,
even though I wanted so badly
to explore what my own queerness meant.

His irises matched my headboard,
and that was enough...
enough for me to know I loved a girl named Blue,
but I wasn't in love with her
like I was in love with him.

His irises matched my headboard,
and it was enough.
Because he was always enough.
My favorite person.

Not because he sits on a pedestal.
Not because of his potential.
But because of how he is...
how he thinks, how he feels.

His irises matched my headboard,
and it was enough...
enough for me to run every scenario through my head,
to validate that what I felt
was the love I deserved,
and not an unhealthy obsession.

Radiant

Let me leave first,
Because I always say goodbye when I do.
In exchange,
I'll let you lead.
You do the asking,
And I do the answering.

My shameful secret?
I love to be asked.
Despite the ways I think in gray,
I answer in black or white.
Yes or no.

Ask me to dance with you.
I'll say yes.
Ask me to go with you.
I'll say yes.
If the magic is there, anyway.

His irises matched my headboard,
And I couldn't look away.
Utterly fixated.

At the expressions on his face.
The way his hands fidgeted,
Picking at his fingers when the nerves came.
The release in his entire body
As he screamed his lungs out.

He's beautiful.

And sure, he's still sad sometimes,
But my god,
He's doing so much better than when I found him.

The sad, beautiful man stepped into his power,
And he is radiant.

The Shift

What if we have sex again?
Do you imagine it...
the fear of what might follow?

We don't kiss now,
and I wonder,
if we did,
would the slow burn be extinguished?

If fear is what you'd even call it...
I don't fear the acts themselves,
or the heartbreak that might follow
in the wake of deep attachment.

I fear the shift in us...
how a kiss might shatter the rhythm,
the way your mind might spiral,
get tangled in its own weight,
and decide we're done.

So, I'm not taking the lead this time.
You take it.
Embrace me.
Dominate me.
Take me home.

Still Soft, Still Kind

We were once like dried flowers,
delicate and preserved,
but you've always been more...
a constant bloom,
weathering every season
with resilience.

This time,
you didn't suffer in silence.
You let the world hear your pain,
and my god, I'm glad you spoke,
glad you're still here to be heard.

Sit with me in your steady light,
not as a beacon of pain,
but of growth.

You've always been radiant,
soft in the way you hold the world,
and kind, even in your boldest moments.

You shine differently now...
still soft, still kind,
and endlessly brilliant.

Baby Girl

Baby girl,
Don't go insane when you spot propaganda
and others don't.
I told you when I revealed my tricks,
my manipulations.

There are some things you cannot unsee,
cannot unlearn.
And it will drive you crazy...
The trade-off with knowledge...
the knowledge of good and evil,
sometimes comes isolation.

The world around us isn't as rosy as we wish it was,
and there's no shame in holding onto hope in humanity...
But when people disappoint, don't let it eat you alive.
Trust that the garden you tend will grow for you.
And even if you're just a ripple of goodness in this world,
your efforts still matter.

Remember when I said...
Burn slowly so you don't burn out.
The world is a better place when you burn bright.
And Blue.

Adore You

I adore you.
You know that, right?
Because time and time again,
as people excluded me from spaces,
you held space for me to just be... me.

You encouraged me to keep writing,
keep creating.
Your eyes glimmered when I showed you new work,
and locked with mine
as I quietly praised you for yours...
because let's be real,
the praise I suppress to be polite is loud.

I adore you,
because you made space for me,
even after meeting my sadistic side.
You sat with me in my discomfort,
and you still do.

You answer the questions
I feel nervous asking,
but safe enough to ask...
because I'm asking you.

You already know I love you,
but I know it's hard for people like us
to really understand what that means
when the love we've known
is wrapped in attachment and heartbreak.

So let me say it first:
I love you.
For you.

I adore you.
For you.

And I have no hesitation about my attachment to you,
because I'd be insane
not to pick you.

The Ugly Cry

I sat before him like a child and wept.
It was embarrassing,
but I felt safe...
safer than I ever felt weeping in front of my father.
More understood than I ever felt with my spouse.
More cared for than I've felt by some of my closest friends.

I wept as the volcano erupted...
grief, embarrassment, shame,
guilt, relief, clarity...
all of it spilling over.

I couldn't explain why
without breaking the dam entirely.
So I excused myself for the ugly cry
and simply told him,
"I'm a Pisces."

Mara

I sent my peace in writing today,
not out of love,
not even out of hope,
but because I'm tired.

Tired of the echoes of her name,
tired of the weight of her shadow.
She's a storm I no longer want to weather,
a thorn in my side
I've finally decided to pull.

This isn't a gesture of kindness.
It's a declaration of surrender.
Not to her,
but to the part of me
that kept fighting battles
long after the war was over.

Mara,
this is my flag raised,
not white with purity,
but stained with exhaustion.

Take it,
leave it,
press it between your palms
or toss it to the wind.

I'm done carrying your name
in my mind,
in my heart,
in the corners of my life
where it no longer belongs.

Mara,
I sent my peace today,
not because you deserved it,
but because I do.

The Reviews Are In

Shut up and dance, like good dancers do.
Be heard, be seen, be funny, be healed...
like good comedians do.

Do this.
Do that.
Be authentic, but not too much.
You're making people uncomfortable.

Be yourself on stage,
but not if yourself is too much.
What's that? You chose to be a character?
Well, that must be who you really are...
Unapproachable.
A threat.
A demon.
A psycho.
Crazy.

The reviews are in:
You couldn't possibly understand this art form.
You're not doing it right.
Do it this way.
No, not that way.
Actually...
just don't do it at all.

Motives

Do you want me to fight for you?
Bare my teeth, as if you're already mine?
Puff my chest, demand they treat you better?
Tell you...
You deserve better?

Trust me,
I'd love to.
But we both know my motives are stained,
self-serving.

So I ask...
Do you want me to do it anyway?
Let my jealousy bleed?
Stand by your side,
as if I have the right to be there?

Or shall we keep this charade?
I cover for you;
you carry on alone,
keeping me hidden,
keeping yourself veiled,
waiting for happiness to find you
like some miracle.

Where do we go from here?
You take the lead.

The Vessel

I told you in the summer,
my enclosure was made of glass,
fragile but smooth, its glaze hiding veins of gold
I never asked for.

By fall, you ran your hands along its surface,
searching for cracks you couldn't see,
testing its strength like an unsteady potter.
You knocked... once, twice...
until the first fracture appeared,
spiderwebbing beneath your fists.

Still, I stayed inside,
watching the lines stretch like molten veins,
each one threatening to break apart the form I called home.

By winter, the glaze was gone,
and you gathered others to help...
forty hands hammering, a blizzard of force.
The glass shattered, raining shards into moss and vines,
sharp as fresh-fired clay breaking against stone.

You **shrieked** when the edges cut your skin,
but I was already crying...
not for you, but for what you destroyed.

The enclosure was unrecognizable:
vines tangled with broken glass,
flowers dusted with shards,
the ground littered with my gilded scars.

So, I left.

The winter wind struck me like kiln heat turned cold,
my feet crunching on fragments that tore into my skin.
Each step bled red into the snow,
but the pain wasn't enough to stop me.
I carried the pieces of my enclosure with me,
embedded in my soles like tiny, gleaming reminders.

And you followed.

You stepped into the broken shell I'd left behind,
expecting something whole, something unbroken.
But you found only ruin...
the cracks too wide for slip to bind,
the shards too sharp for your hands.

Still, you came after me,
your voice sharp as a chisel against ice,
calling me a beast...
something feral, something that had escaped.

But I am not an animal.

I am the vessel you shattered,
the pottery you never learned to shape,
the cracks you couldn't repair.

It is winter, and I do not hide.

The shards still glint in my feet,
a patina of pain gilded by frost.
Each step presses them deeper,
but I press forward all the same.

You watch from the edges of the snow,
your hands raw from the cold,

and I wonder if you see me now...
the vessel I've become.

The Resistance Begins in Bed

Join me in the resistance.
Not with guns or cannons,
nor knives, nor bombs.

Just words.
Pattern recognition.
Adaptable planning.

I told you in the fall:
they'd be back...
the administration that stripped us
of autonomy,
littered our streets
with lifeless bodies,
left our forms
hollowed, fractured,
stripped of abilities
we once claimed as ours.

Join me in the resistance from bed,
on the days when rising feels impossible,
when every ache screams louder
than resolve.

Tap your phone.
Press your truth into pixels.

Join me in the resistance from burnout,
where exhaustion makes its home.

Let's talk prose,
weave rhymes,
shape language into armor.

Strengthen our minds,
fortify our souls,
as we prepare to repair these bodies
to grow stronger
for the time when words must rise,
when silence
can no longer hold.

Built for Pleasure

The room hums low with secrets,
soft shadows wrapping around us.
A Polaroid clicks, the moment freezes,
your hands framing me like art:
a masterpiece of flesh and desire.

You tilt my chin, command my gaze,
lips brushing mine in stolen whispers.
A growl catches wicked in your throat
as teeth meet skin, marking me as yours.
Salt and surrender flood my senses,
the air electric with the push and pull
of power exchanged and freely given.

"You're built for pleasure," you murmur,
like it's a fact etched into my bones.
I arch into you, trembling,
your control both torment and sanctuary.
You tease me to the edge, hold me there,
taunting, testing, tasting.
Relentless. Relentless and mine.

The Polaroid snaps again: evidence
of how far you've taken me,
how far I'll go just to stay in your hands.
Your body presses me deeper
into a space where time dissolves,
and the only thing left is us.

When it's over, I'm all jagged breaths,
bruised hips, bitten lips,
and the fingerprints you've left on my soul.
You kiss me then, slow and soft,
not as my tormentor, but my salvation.

The Polaroids scatter, a secret only for us,
proof that I am yours.

I Bought Him Clothes

I bought him clothes,
replacements for the necessities
and the creature comforts lost.

I stood by his side
as we watched his world burn,
smoke billowing from the roof,
extinguished by the weight of water
heavy enough to cave in the floors.

I embraced him.
A few times...
and told him I was relieved
that he and his tiny tabby are okay.
I know that's not all that matters,
but it's what matters most.

I bought him clothes
to show my support,
to provide him with stability
stripped from him in an instant,
with a bang and a spark
before the smoke took over.

I showed him the kindness
and support of which he is worthy,
and for the first time,
he let me.

I bought him clothes,
because clothes are replaceable,
but he isn't.

And my god,
I'm grateful
that he's alive.

Eyes Burn

I think about us often...
the way impulse felt so free,
under hot weather
and sunlight streaming through my windows.

Do you remember?
Kissing my lips,
listening as I nervously apologized
about my breath after eating,
and you just didn't care.

Primal.
Dripping with desire,
rooted in understanding.

I stripped myself bare for you:
body, soul, everything I was.
I wanted to let go,
to feel unbound,
to watch your eyes burn
with that fire in your irises
as you claimed every inch of me.

Do you ever revisit the scene?
Those intimate moments,
where desire softened
into tired slumber,
where our breaths mingled
and the night stood still,
holding its breath with us?

Seasons have come and gone,
yet you hold my attention...
soft, beautiful, sad,

and just...
fucking real.

How do you move on
when you don't want to?
When you tried,
and found that others
don't compare?

I bide my time,
quietly bidding for your affection.
Does it bother you...
to be so close
and still keep your distance?

Pellets to the Rats

Did I get the job done?
Bare my teeth?
Puff my chest out?
Just enough to take the heat off of you?

Indifference breeds cruelty,
And there is no cruelty sharper
Than that of a woman
Who watches the wolves salivate
As you cling to the edge of The Well.

She cuts the ivy,
Turns venom into bait,
And throws pellets to the rats,
Their hunger redirected,
Their teeth dull with confusion.

I keep them distracted,
Let them gnaw on their own weakness,
While I reach for your hands,
Pull you back up,
And remind the beasts below
They were never a match for us.

The Cretaceous Period

Do you think the T-Rex ever worried
about its place in history?
Or did it simply **exist**,
chasing smaller things,
crushing bones between its teeth,
roaring into a sky that
was already planning its extinction?

The eel does not ask these questions.
It moves in the dark,
slips through water,
slithers across land when it has to.
It does not need permission to survive.

The iris does not mourn what came before.
It was here when the world belonged to giants.
It watched meteors fall,
saw the first hands reach to pluck it,
and it bloomed anyway.

The amethyst spent millions of years underground,
unshaped, unseen, unbothered.
Then one day, the earth split open,
and someone decided it was beautiful.

Some things survive.
Not because they fight.
Not because they run.
But because they simply **are.**

Maybe we should be so lucky.

His Favorite

I did your favorite position with him.
I never told him why.
Never let the words slip,
never let the truth settle
between the sheets.

I just gave instructions,
a whispered directive,
a shift of weight,
a tilt of my hips...
just right, just like that,
just the way you like it.

And he thought it was for me.
Maybe, in a way, it was.
A lesson. A study. A test.
I wanted to know what it felt like,
to be taken the way you take,
to be held in the shape of your pleasure.

And when it was over?
I knew.

It wasn't the angle.
It wasn't the motion.
It wasn't even the act itself.

It was you.
Your presence.
Your hands.
Your voice.
The way you ruin me
without even touching me.

And now?
Now, I sit with it,
holding onto the secret,
waiting to tell you...
just to watch what you do with it.

A Moment to Process

Don't mistake my silence for indifference.
I just need a moment to process.

If you see me run,
Don't assume it's because I'm disinterested.
I just need a moment to process.

If the invitation falls from my lips,
And I pause before offering the subtle cue
That I am not in charge of this dynamic.
Know that I just need a moment to process.

Does it seem like I stopped fighting for you?
I did.
I put in the work,
And if you want me,
You'll decide that for yourself.
I already made it easy.

Don't miscalculate my stillness.
Every good Machiavellian knows...
If you want a job done right,
You get someone else to do the dirty work
for you.

Everything You're Worth

I want to take you for everything that you're worth.
Because I lost more.

My sanity.
My marriage.
My home.
My reputation.
My business.
My money.
My time.

I want to take you for everything that you're worth.
Because you knew better.
And it pains me to say that you didn't...
In order to keep the peace.

Waiting

The air hums thick with silence,
a hush between the storm's breath
and the world waking up again.

My clothes cling like second skin,
rain tracing lazy rivers down my arms,
soaking into fabric, into flesh,
into the spaces I keep to myself.

The green is electric:
more alive in the damp,
lush in a way only water can reveal.
Leaves glisten like polished jade,
the earth dark and breathing beneath me.

A bird perches in the tangle of branches,
feathers puffed, soaked in waiting.
It does not shake the rain away,
does not rush to be dry...
just sits, just exists,
just listens.

And I, too, linger in the stillness,
not racing toward comfort,
not running from the weight of water...
but feeling it settle into me,
into everything I already know.

Legacy

How do you think we'll be remembered?
Will they carve our names in stone,
or will we live only in the echoes
of those who knew us best?

Iris moved like a story still being written,
every step deliberate, every silence a choice.
He loved war, but only if he won.
Loyal in the way the best soldiers were:
cautious, calculated, the kind you followed
even when you shouldn't.

Blue danced where the world was quiet,
where the floor creaked beneath the weight of devotion.
She bent herself into beauty, into discipline,
held balance like a secret between trembling hands.

Mara held history like a contract,
terms and conditions set in ink,
proof that every battle was real,
every scar accounted for.
She stood when others didn't.

Ivy ran first, thought later,
too fast to catch, too stubborn to quit.
She loved like a wildfire,
burned like one too.

And then there was Cissy.
5'5".
Taller in heels...
and bad at math.

Living Renaissance

You're a love letter in motion,
  A living Renaissance.

May I take your portrait?
Accent your curves
with oil and pigment,
Turn you into
my personal giclée?

Chemical

May I take your portrait?
Invite you into the darkroom,
show you in real time how you look through my lens?

Would you join me where the only light is red,
where your silhouette sharpens in the hush,
where my hands move with precision,
steady, deliberate...
focused on you?

Is it still romantic
even though the scent of developer is putrid,
clinging to our skin, sour and sharp?
Would you be tempted to kiss me anyway,
press against me,
taste the chemical burn on my lips?

I could show you the image before it sets,
your face soft in the rinse,
the moment suspended between us.

Or you could touch me now,
before the picture dries,
before the chemicals lose their bite.

False Spring

It's strange how the seasons have changed in my lifetime.
Snow fell twice in Atlanta just weeks ago,
and today, it's 77 degrees.

February 7th.
Magnolias and camellias are blooming.
The air smells like spring...
but it isn't.

It reminds me of the first time I fell deeply in love.
Fall, 2007.
The world has changed, and so have I.

I turn 32 soon.
And if this were a leap year,
it would be our anniversary.
But it isn't.

And the rings aren't on our fingers anymore.

An amethyst pendant hangs near my heart,
the stone of the seventh chakra,
the crown.

Strange, isn't it?
How a false spring can still feel so real...

I hope you don't mind that I miss you.

But when the moon is full,
it's harder to pretend I don't.

Good Girls Don't Haunt

Good girls don't leave shadows.
They slip out quiet, like a ribbon untied,
folding themselves into memory,
soft, untroubling, gone.

Good wives don't linger.
They pack their bags neatly,
leave the ring on the nightstand,
walk away with grace...
never with ghosts in their lungs,
never with hands that still itch
for the lock on a door
they swore they'd never knock on again.

Good daughters don't haunt their own pasts,
don't stand in the wreckage of old homes,
old loves, old selves,
sifting through the ash like there's still something to find.

But I do.

I left, but I never fully left.
I danced away, but the music still calls me back.
I unhooked the chains, but the weight still lingers,
settling in my bones,
shadowing my steps.

They say if you aren't a good girl,
at least be a martyr.
At least be noble in your suffering.
At least make it clean.

But I am not clean.
I am not free.

I am still here,
somewhere between escape and return,
between mourning and moving on,
between being the girl who left
and the woman who is still haunted.

Not About You *(His Perspective)*

I'm not saying this is about you.
I'm just saying...
if someone *were* to write a poem about someone *like* you,
they'd probably start with your eyes,
because people always start with eyes.
But that feels obvious.
Lazy.
You'd make fun of me for that.

So, instead, I'll start with how you always know
exactly when to look at me.
Not just in the normal, everyday way...
but in the way that makes me forget
what I was about to say next.
Which is inconvenient, honestly.
Especially for a guy whose whole thing
is knowing what to say next.

And maybe they'd write about how you talk,
the way your voice slows down
right before you say something that'll stick
in my head for three days longer than it should.
Or how you laugh...
not the polite one you give to other people,
but the real one, the sharp one,
the one you try to hide behind your drink.
The one that makes me feel like I got away with something.

If someone *were* to write that poem,
they might admit...
just for a second,
just between the lines...
that they think about you more than they should.
That maybe, when they leave early,

it's not just because of a long day
or a bad set
or whatever excuse works best.

But like I said,
this isn't that poem.
I don't write poems.
That's your thing.
I just know that if I did...
if I ever did...
it might sound a little bit like this.

But, again.
Not about you.

Fine, Then. *(Her Perspective)*

I wasn't going to write about you.
I had other things to do.
Important things, probably.
But then you had to go and say,
"If I were the type to write a poem."
Like it wasn't already too late.

So now, here I am,
sitting with your words
and the space you leave when you go.
I should be used to it by now.
And maybe I am.
Or maybe I just know how to
make something of the absence.

I could tell you that I don't notice when you leave,
but you'd know I'm lying.
I count the seconds afterward.
Not to keep you... just to see
how long it takes for the room to shift.

I could say I don't read into things,
but we both know that isn't true either.
I read between the pauses.
I read between your bad excuses.
I read between your *Not About Yous*
and your half-closed doors.

And I could say I won't write about this.
That I'll leave it alone,
let it sit, let it settle.
But we both know that was never an option.
You should've known better

than to start a poem
and expect me not to finish it.

Somewhere, In Another Life

Somewhere, in another life,
we didn't fuck this up.

Not because we met at a better time...
we got that part right.
But because love stayed easy,
or at least, it stayed.

Because we never had to learn
what "worse" really meant.
Because distance never settled in
between people who once knew each other like home.

Somewhere, in another life,
we got it right.

But not in this one.
Not in the life where we stayed long enough
to find out what falling apart feels like.
Not in the life where trying harder
was never going to be enough.

There is no wondering,
no "what if,"
no question left to ask.
We stayed.
We learned.
And for better or for worse...
we got worse.

Pistol

I already told my mama about you.
I told her that if it works out,
she better prepare her husband.

Because this time,
I'm not bringing home a passive peacekeeper
like my last husband.

I'm bringing home a pistol.

Nostalgia

There is something nostalgic about your presence.
I'm not sure if it's your boyish charm,
or if it's the way I told my husband about you,
just like I told my daddy about my first boyfriend.

Not seeking permission.
Just stating my love as fact.

She Glows

She's moving like laughter,
like a song she forgot she knew,
like the weight she carried for so long
just slipped off her shoulders mid-spin.

Same bodysuit, same braids,
same favorite socks pulled high...
but she looks different.
Younger.
Like the girl she used to be
has finally come home to her.

Her partner stays wrapped up,
full sweats, steady, grounded.
Tiff is all light, all ease...
dancing with the kind of joy
that doesn't check itself in the mirror first,
that doesn't ask permission to exist.

She lands soft, laughing.
Not for the crowd, not for the camera...
just because it feels good.

And that's it.
That's the thing.
She looks like it finally feels *good* to be her.

Conditional

I told the man I married
I loved him after six months.

I've known you for eight.

Frankly, I loved you both.
From day one.

Because I'm the type of girl
who falls in love at first sight.

"I love you,"
he said,
buried in my body,
in our shared bed.

"I love you, too,"
I replied...
but I wasn't sure if I meant it.
Or how I meant it.

We were married at the time.
Objectively, I knew I did,
and I knew he did too.

But it didn't feel the same.
Outside the bedroom,
neither of us said it.

Come to Confess

Do you want to keep it casual,
or do you want more?
I can feel the hunger in you...
it matches mine.

Come to my place.
Fall into me.
See if you fall in love.

Would you pray to me?
Would you worship with your hands,
your mouth,
your body...
as if I were the altar
where you confessed your sins?

Daisy

He loves me.
She tattooed it to me with care,
where I am most vulnerable,
where I carry the weight of the world,
as if it is fact.

Cissy means sixth,
and we can all count.
Six petals.
Two options.

He loves me.
He loves me not.

If he's a Gatsby,
what does that make me?

Remember When?

Remember when life was just... easy?
I know we didn't think it was back then...
because yeah, life has always been hard on people like us.

But remember when dance was just dance?
Heels were just heels?
And we just... got along?

Remember when *I do* meant *'til death*?
In sickness and in health?
And then I got sick enough that
I do became *I'm done...*

Luna

He gave me butterflies today,
basking in the evening glow of the coffeehouse.
He was radiant.
His irises. His smile.
The way the light kissed his cheeks,
lingered on the tip of his nose.

I tried to stay grounded...
anchored by the scent of espresso and warm air...
but truth be told, I was already floating.
Inching toward him like a magnet,
like something inevitable.

He gave me butterflies today,
and I told him I'd trade...
one moth for countless butterflies.
A fair exchange, I think.

Wax & Wane

How do you think we'll be remembered?
Will they carve our names in stone,
or will we live only in the echoes
of those who knew us best?

Iris moves like a story still being written,
every step deliberate, every silence a choice.
He loves war, but only if he wins.
Loyal in the way the best soldiers are...
cautious, calculated, the kind you follow
even when you shouldn't.

Daisy waits, petals pressed in permanence,
a name inked where the world is heaviest.
She counts her chances like omens,
a gambler in a game where love is currency,
but the house always wins.

Mara holds history like a contract,
terms and conditions set in ink,
proof that every battle was real,
every scar accounted for.
She stands when others don't.

Ivy runs first, thinks later,
too fast to catch, too stubborn to quit.
She loves like a wildfire,
burns like one too.

Luna drifts between light and shadow,
a pale-winged ghost drawn to the glow.
She does not flinch when the flames rise...
some creatures were never meant for daylight.

Blue dances where the world is quiet,
where devotion creaks beneath its weight.
She bends into beauty, into discipline,
holds balance like a secret between trembling hands.

And then there is Cissy.
5'5".
Taller in heels.
Bad at math.
But good at this.

Together, we melt into wax,
a shifting shape, an undying flame.
Not carved in stone,
but pressed into memory,
sealed in the spaces
where we lived.

Kindling

Not all fires are meant to burn wild.
Some are set with purpose...
a controlled burn,
clearing what was,
making space for what could be.

I have walked through fields of irises
rising from the ash,
held hands with ghosts,
laughed at the impossible.

They say only men become prophets,
but I have seen the lights,
felt the weight of knowing.
And when fire rains,
I will not be absent.

This time, it will be a controlled burn.
This time, I will stay.

Blank

Do you worry...
that one day, I'll look at you
and the light in my eyes will fade?

You know the one.

When the sun hits my amber irises,
and my pupils swell,
and all you see in your peripherals
is the glimmer on the surface.

When I stare at you like a painting,
breaking you down by hue,
by texture, by lightness, by dark.

Observing you.
Consuming you.

Do you worry...
that one day, I'll look at you,
and your canvas will be just...
blank?

32

Tomorrow's my birthday, ya know?
Thirty-two.

Three years since I spent my birthday with you.

I don't want to make a big deal out of it.
No party.
No balloons.
No grand vacation.
No restaurant reservations.

Just me.
The mountain.
And the moon.

Happy Birthday

There she goes.
Cissy Stag.
32 years old.
5K left in the bank,
nothing in savings.
5'5",
taller in heels.

Bad at math,
small compared to her debt.
Great at pattern recognition.
Younger,
and skinnier in this photo.

Isn't she radiant?
Just because she's alive...

What If?

What if we have sex again?
Would it settle the question
or write the last line of a story
I wasn't ready to finish?

Would we leave fulfilled,
content in knowing,
or would satisfaction itself
become the reason we crave more?

What if the night means nothing...
just heat, just hands,
a moment taken, tested,
then tucked away in the past?

I don't fear the act itself.
Not the weight of your body,
not the way you move inside me.
I fear waking up
and knowing, without question,
that there's nothing left to wonder.

So maybe we try.
Maybe we see for ourselves.
Maybe it's just once.
Maybe it's nothing.
Or maybe, just maybe,
one night is how the story ends.

Balance

Your presence is enough,
always has been,
a steady force in the ebb and flow,
a warmth I never need to question.
But I wonder,
is mine enough for you?

Am I the friend you see,
or just a love bomb waiting to explode,
a potential partner to untangle,
rather than someone to stand beside you
without the weight of expectation?

I'm caught between the push and pull...
your distance, my reach,
wondering if the spaces between us
are filled with doubt or desire.
Do you see me for who I am,
or is there something more you expect
that I can't give?

I don't want to swing on this tightrope,
swaying between what's real
and what's imagined,
between the warmth of connection
and the cold fear of being more than a friend
just because my presence fills a void.

I offer what I can...
not in the hope of romance,
but in the belief that true friendship is enough,
that being seen as I am, without pressure,
is all I need.

Yet, I'm left wondering,
when you step back,
if I've failed to be enough,
or if the space between us
will always leave me guessing.

Let's Go to Neverland Together

Sometimes, I forget we're not children.
Your eyes are bright,
girlish charm in a grown-up frame.
We dance and sing,
and for a moment,
we take flight...
weightless, shadowless.

Cathedral

We spoke for the first time today...
...after God knows how long.
It was simple,
like stepping into confession.

Wild

If I am being honest with myself,
I don't know why he runs.
I don't know why he sleeps with one eye open but pretends
to rest...
always observing,
testing my boundaries.
What am I willing to give?
How accommodating will I be for him?
I love him, but...
he runs when I express love.
Not just for him,
but for her.

I don't know if it's jealousy,
or if he assumes he is my only muse these days.
I wrote...
mountains and mountains of words...
to win him back.
And it worked!
Kind of.
He came back,
but he still doesn't know how to hold me,
how to help me feel properly cared for...
in any role.

I fear he sees me as forever potential,
never present,
never a true friend to give or receive invitation.
I can see him...
he's RIGHT THERE,
but a pane of glass keeps us separate.
Not mine.
His.

The Enclosure was never meant for me.
I was always meant to run wild.

Snapshot

I wish you were here,
so I could watch you in the light where I'm sitting.
The day is perfect:
seventy-something degrees,
clear skies,
birds singing.
A breeze lifts the baby hairs framing my face,
gentle, never too much.

I wish I could see you...
seated on the ground,
pine needles scattered around you,
your back resting against the trunk of a tree.
Maybe the ducks would catch your eye,
or maybe you'd glance down at your phone,
start writing,
crack a smile at something only you understand.

And I'd just look at you,
memorizing this moment,
pressing it deep into my mind.
And think...
God, I'm so in love with you.

Melt

I can feel it now.
Your hands fumbling at the base of my neck,
aiming to latch a hook through a wire,
placing this necklace around me...
a quiet claim.

I can feel it now.
The slight heat of your breath,
held tight behind your lips,
as your hands push my hair forward.

And for a moment, I wonder...
will you lean closer,
kiss me softly,
and be ready to catch me
when I melt in your arms?

I Sold My Car Today

I sold my car today,
and replaced her with something to her likeness...
older, well-traveled,
a brighter shade of green.

I fought to keep her,
clung to the weight of what she meant,
but when the time came,
I knew.

And I love this one even more.
173K miles, but plenty left to go,
rebuilt, steady, running like new.
Yet something about her feels classic...
solid, original, meant to be.

I sold my car today
and quietly honored my wedding anniversary,
my freedom date.
And for once...
for the first time in a long time...
I celebrated being seen,
being heard.

Loudly.

Break My Heart

Break my heart in any role.
I promise,
It's easy.
Easy to look beyond my humanity
To see the monster in me then
that you still see in yourself now.
Break my heart by never accepting me.
Keeping me at arm's length.
Looking to me for a source of comfort,
And growing angry with me for thinking that I matter to you
because you do.

Close

Don't be surprised if you arrive
expecting a rejection,
And I pull you in close.
Squish you just a little bit.
And refuse to apologize for violating your space
after you violated my trust.
I love you.
You know that, right?
I've said it for a long time now.
From rock bottom.
Through my own recovery.
My love for you... Hell... I don't think it's unrequited at this
point,
But I am certain that it is unconditional.
Because if there is a way that I can fight for
understanding.
For comfort.
For feeling like home... even though we both have a
skewed idea of what homes should feel like...
Yeah.
I'll fight for that.

Rings

I still have the rings.
Not in some secret place,
stowed away for safekeeping.
They're scattered on my desk,
mixed with opened mail
and other miscellaneous things.

Sometimes, I still wear them
on my right hand, though.

Not all good things last forever,
and marriage is no exception.
Sometimes, people grow apart.
And in time, you learn that the vows you took
were easier said than kept.

So, hold your people tight.
A little affection
goes a long way for lonely hearts.

The Exhibit

We're returning to the scene of the wreckage this spring,
where The Enclosure once stood.
Are you ready?
I am.

Here's how I think it will go:
We will kneel in the ruins together,
sort the shards by color, by size,
wash them clean, brush away the dust.
We will fit the largest pieces into patterns,
watch light spill through them in fractured blues and golds.

The slivers too small to place
we will crush into glitter,
like the shimmer of a century ago.

And with the last of the cold, the tether will dissolve.
What once enclosed us will no longer exist,
but the exhibit will remain:
not a cage, but a window.

When the final piece is set,
we will step back, look through,
and trust that we can exist,
not as reflections, not as ghosts,
but as people, beneath the same sun.

To Your Likeness

I miss you.
You get that, right?
I wish that I felt confident that you feel the same.
I miss you, and I drowned my sorrows in the feeling,
Until a man to your likeness offered me a welcome
distraction.
You two don't really look all that much alike,
But kissing him felt familiar.
Like I was kissing you.
I took him home,
And we had sex.
Caring, safe, intimate sex
So much so that I didn't notice that he'd left bite marks on
my body until this morning.
We snuggled afterwards, and I wished him goodnight.
I'll see you when I see you I said.
And frankly,
I don't have a clue if I will ever see him again.
I just know that in those moments,
He felt like you.
Same wit. Same innocence. And fearless like you...
When we first met at least.
I woke this morning with a pit in my stomach,
Because yes, I had fun.
Like consenting adults do.
But God, I'm not even waiting on a text from him.
Because I'm too worried that you won't understand
when you hear what happened...
When my name rolls off the tongues of the people we
know...
Because I met him in our shared space.
After telling you that we needed to take a break from sharing
it.

Divorced

I got divorced today,
And it was a surprise.
Kind of.
I saw the paperwork,
But I didn't really know what it meant.
Just nodded my head and said thank you.
And just like that,
It was done.
This big decision.
One that I went back and forth about for six months
after saying I was done.
I love him now.
I'll love him forever.
But honestly...
I deserved so much more than what I got after saying, "I do."

Go

What if I actually go with you?
Would that be okay?
Would you trust it?
Even if it never meant settling down?
Even if we never had sex?
Never even kissed?
Would it be enough for me to be your companion?
Just because I crave adventure,
And I know that I'd prefer to not go alone.

Sinatra

Two weeks.
That is all it took for me to grow excited...
And recognize that it wouldn't work...
Despite the deep intimacy...
And frankly... I wish that it broke my heart differently.
But it didn't.
In his truth lied mine...
I always get attached...
DEEPLY...
And you stood the test of time.

Temple

Baby girl,
Don't think for a second that you are unworthy.
Unlovable.
Undesirable.
We all know who comes to your temple to worship.

Turnips

When we garden,
Let us not forget that it's not only flowers that grow.
Flowers are beautiful and give life to other plants,
But alone, they are only that... beautiful.
In our garden, we grow strawberries.
Tomatoes.
Turnips.
And trust that while the surface may bloom in spring,
The soil remains rich with life through winter.
Sustainable.

Real

When does the world finally feel real to you?
Is it on days that rain falls,
And the trees become greener?
What about on nights when the wind blows,
And you pump gasoline in blinding light?
Do you feel real when you go barefoot?
What about when you lie naked in bed?
When you sing with a friend?
Dance with a lover?
Do you feel real when you finally feel safe?
Or do you only feel real when you suffer?

Foolish

I don't start wars,
But I don't lose them either.
All is fair in love and war, you say?
Only a foolish romantic would believe that.

Tides

Bleed and bear witness to the moon in her glory.
She is stone-cold.
She does not burn.
She does not blind.
But do not underestimate her.
We all know who pulls the tides.

Don't Call

I didn't think it would be this hard.
Fighting for the bare minimum.
Not love.
Respect.
Call me crazy.
Call me obsessed.
Just don't call me until I've recovered.

Collapse

I hope that this is my turning point.
The one that sobers my mind.
My heart.
And makes peace with my loneliness.
His irises matched my headboard,
And it wasn't enough.
Because I was always too much.
For him anyway.
Not a lover.
Not a friend.
Not an acquaintance.
Just someone who I choose to no longer know.

Don't Write

Don't write me as your muse or your monster.
The role is well-worn and worn out.
Write me like I'm right here.
With you.
Present.

Soft

Baby girl, are you ready to grow soft?
I've seen the fire in your eyes...
The way your pupils grow large and frighten those who cross
you...
I've seen you through love and loss.
Held you when no one else would... or could... because they
didn't know how.

Baby girl, I've seen your heart harden.
I've watched those around you play with it as it grew softer...
More malleable.

Baby girl, are you ready to grow soft?
And trust that you're safe enough for softness this time?

Here stands Cissy Stag...
5'5"
Barefoot
And worthy of beautiful life... even if she leaves no legacy.

About the Author

Cissy Stag is the author of *Stripped, Tethered,* and now *Wax.* Her work blends personal mythology, queerness, and survival into poetry that holds nothing back. She lives in Atlanta with her beloved rabbit, Echeveria.